W9-BLM-807

What's So Great About . . . ?

ELIZABETH BLACKWELL

Amie Jane Leavitt

Mitchell Lane
PUBLISHERS

P.O. Box 196
Hockessin, Delaware 19707
Visit us on the web: www.mitchelllane.com
Comments? email us: mitchelllane@mitchelllane.com

Printing   1   2   3   4   5   6   7   8   9

A Robbie Reader/What's So Great About . . . ?

Amelia Earhart	Anne Frank	Annie Oakley
Christopher Columbus	Daniel Boone	Davy Crockett
Elizabeth Blackwell	Ferdinand Magellan	Francis Scott Key
Galileo	George Washington Carver	Harriet Tubman
Helen Keller	Henry Hudson	Jacques Cartier
Johnny Appleseed	Paul Bunyan	Robert Fulton
Rosa Parks	Sam Houston	

Library of Congress Cataloging-in-Publication Data
Leavitt, Amie Jane.
  Elizabeth Blackwell / by Amie Jane Leavitt.
    p. cm. — (A Robbie reader)
  Includes bibliographical references and index.
  ISBN-13: 978-1-58415-579-9 (library bound)
  1. Blackwell, Elizabeth, 1821-1910. 2. Women physicians—Biography. I. Title.
  R154.B623L43 2007
  610.92—dc22
  [B]
                                                                              2007000810

ABOUT THE AUTHOR: Amie Jane Leavitt is a versatile and accomplished author, editor, and photographer. A Brigham Young University graduate, she has written dozens of books for kids, has contributed to online and print media, and has worked as a consultant, writer, and editor for numerous educational publishing and assessment companies. Ms. Leavitt is a former teacher who has taught all subjects and grade levels. She enjoys gathering exciting tales for her writing and photographing beautiful scenery as she travels. Ms. Leavitt particularly enjoyed researching and writing this book on Elizabeth Blackwell. Dr. Blackwell's achievements prove that regardless of obstacles, everyone can fulfill his or her dreams.

PHOTO CREDITS: Cover, pp. 1, 3, 4, 8, 16, 24—Schlesinger Library; pp. 6, 7, 18, 22—National Library of Medicine; p. 11—Getty Images; p. 12—Library of Congress; pp. 21, 27—Barbara Marvis.

TABLE OF CONTENTS

Words in **bold** type can be found in the glossary.

In 1845, after years of teaching, Elizabeth Blackwell decided to become a doctor—something no woman in the United States had done before.

Graduation Day

January 23, 1849, was a special day at New York's Geneva Medical College. It was **graduation** (grad-joo-WAY-shun) day. Students finish school and graduate every year. So why was this day so important? That day, the first woman ever to attend and complete medical school received her **diploma** (dih-PLOH-muh). Her name was Elizabeth Blackwell.

People crowded into the large Presbyterian (pres-buh-TEER-ee-un) church early. Women packed into the balconies, and men stood in the aisles. They all wanted "to see a lady receive a medical diploma," as one of Elizabeth's brothers wrote in a letter home.

The music started playing, and the graduates entered the church. People gave

Elizabeth's diploma opened many doors not only for Blackwell but for all women everywhere.

speeches. Then Elizabeth's name was called. She walked up to the stage in her black silk graduation gown. As she approached, the school's president rose from his seat. He smiled and handed her a piece of paper—her diploma. She said, "Sir, I thank you; it shall be the effort of my life, with the help of the Most High, to shed honor on my diploma." The audience clapped and cheered.

Later, a professor spoke about Elizabeth. He said that she had studied hard. She had

The Presbyterian church in Geneva, New York, was packed the day Elizabeth Blackwell graduated from Geneva Medical College. The people wanted to see the first woman receive a degree in medicine.

proved she belonged there. Now, she was graduating at the top of her class. Elizabeth was proud of her achievements.

Many women are doctors today, but in the 1800s, people didn't believe women could do this kind of job. Elizabeth had shown the world that these **opinions** (oh-PIN-yuns) were wrong. Women doctors today can thank Elizabeth Blackwell for her accomplishments. She was a pioneer in the field of medicine.

7

In her later years, Elizabeth fondly remembered her childhood in Bristol, England. She would return to England many times as an adult to practice and teach medicine.

Life in Bristol

Elizabeth Blackwell was born on February 3, 1821, in Bristol, England. She was the third child of Samuel and Hannah Blackwell. She had eight brothers and sisters. "It was a great advantage to have been born one of a large family group of healthy, active children, surrounded by wholesome influences," Elizabeth wrote in 1895.

Elizabeth had a fun childhood. She loved to play outside with her brothers and sisters in the garden near their home. "To active, imaginative children this little domain was a source of never-ending enjoyment, whether cherishing pet animals, cultivating gardens, or playing Robinson Crusoe," she wrote.

All of the Blackwell children were smart and **determined** (dee-TER-mihnd). Out of all of them, Elizabeth was the most strong-willed. Many people said she was just like her father. When she wanted to do something, she didn't stop until she had done it well.

Samuel Blackwell was a successful businessman. He owned a factory that processed sugar. Samuel did not think as other people did during his time period. Many people agreed with **slavery** (SLAY-vree). He didn't. Many people thought men and women could not do the same things. Samuel didn't. He thought women should have the same rights and opportunities as men. Many people also thought that only boys should go to school. Samuel wanted his sons and his daughters to learn the same things. He hired a private teacher to give them lessons. They all learned history, Greek, Latin, math, grammar, and French together.

In 1831, England was in an uproar. Some of the workers were angry because of conditions in factories. They set buildings on

Elizabeth was the third child in a family of nine brothers and sisters. She was always grateful to be part of a large family.

fire. They damaged property. Samuel was afraid his home and business would be next. He sold everything he owned and bought tickets for his family to go to America. Elizabeth was only eleven years old.

"In the month of August, 1832, the family party of eight children and seven adults sailed from Bristol in the merchant ship *Cosmo*," she recalled. The ship reached New York about seven weeks later.

William Lloyd Garrison was a well-known abolitionist of this time period. He became a good friend of the Blackwells and was a frequent visitor in their New Jersey home.

CHAPTER THREE

Hard Times

The Blackwells lived in New York City first. Then they moved across the Hudson River to New Jersey. Samuel started another sugar factory there.

During this time, Elizabeth and her siblings enjoyed going to special clubs and meetings. They especially liked listening to the words of William Lloyd Garrison. Slavery was still practiced in the United States, and Garrison was an **abolitionist** (aa-buh-LIH-shuh-nist). He believed slavery was wrong. Elizabeth and her family agreed with him.

Life went well for the family for a few years. Then, in 1836, the sugar factory caught fire. Samuel's business went up in flames.

Slaves worked in horrible conditions in Caribbean sugar mills. Elizabeth and her family "gave up the use of sugar" since it was a slave product.

The Blackwells had to start over again. This time, they moved to Cincinnati (sin-sih-NAA-tee), Ohio. They opened another factory there. They wanted to grow sugar beets. If more sugar were made from beets, fewer slaves would be needed on sugarcane plantations. But the family's troubles weren't over. During their first summer in Ohio, Samuel became very ill. After several days, he died.

The family was extremely sad and missed their father very much. They were also scared. Samuel had just started the Ohio factory, so he had very little money saved when he died. How would the family buy food and pay for their house?

As Elizabeth later wrote: "The three elder sisters set to work, and in time established a day and boarding school for young ladies." The sisters taught lessons in the subjects they had learned as children. Elizabeth also taught piano lessons. "For the next few years, until the younger children grew up and were able gradually to share in the work, we managed to support the family and maintain a home."

Elizabeth liked helping her family, but she didn't really like teaching. There were very few jobs a woman could have in the 1800s. She could work as a teacher, maid, nurse, or factory worker. Women were expected to get married and raise children, not work at jobs. Elizabeth was still young and didn't want to get married yet. She didn't like the idea of doing any of those jobs, either. She struggled to figure out what she should do with her life.

Elizabeth Blackwell believed that her achievements benefited all women everywhere. She once said: "For what is done or learned by one class of women becomes, by virtue of their common womanhood, the property of all women."

Dr. Blackwell

In 1845, Elizabeth's friend, Mary, was very sick and near death. Elizabeth visited her often. One day, Mary told Elizabeth that she should become a doctor. She thought Elizabeth was smart and good with people. "If I could have been treated by a lady doctor, my worst sufferings would have spared me," Mary said.

At first, Elizabeth didn't think becoming a doctor was a good idea. Yet as she thought about it more, she decided Mary might be right. There weren't any female doctors. Elizabeth liked to help people. Maybe this is what she should do with her life.

Elizabeth started reading books about **medicine** (MEH-dih-sin). The more she read,

When Geneva Medical College accepted Elizabeth Blackwell, it became the first medical school in the United States to admit a woman. In 1871 the college became part of Syracuse University. It is known today as the State University of New York Upstate Medical University.

the more she liked it. She decided to apply to medical school. She applied to twenty-eight schools. All of them gave her the same answer: No. Women could not be doctors, they said. Many people thought Elizabeth should forget about her plan and do something else. Other people thought she should just dress up like a boy, because a girl would never be allowed to go to medical school.

Elizabeth refused to give up. At last, the Geneva Medical College in New York accepted her. The students there had taken a vote. They all agreed that Elizabeth should be able to study with them. She began classes in 1847. It took her two years to finish. Her dream of becoming a doctor was finally coming true.

After college, Elizabeth decided to move to Paris, France. She wanted to become a **surgeon** (SUR-jun). She worked at a **clinic** (KLIH-nik) in Paris and watched the surgeons operate on patients.

One day at the clinic, Elizabeth was helping a baby with an eye infection. Today, this illness is easy to cure. A person just has to take special medicines and the eye gets better. But in the 1800s, there weren't any medicines to help this type of infection. While she was washing the baby's eye, "some of the water had spurted into my eye," Elizabeth remembered. Soon, her eye became swollen. She had caught the infection.

Elizabeth stayed in bed for several weeks with cold rags on her face. The doctors gave

Once she became a doctor, Elizabeth gave many lectures to other women who wanted to become doctors.

her special treatments. None of them helped. Elizabeth's eye became so diseased that she could no longer see. It had to be replaced with a glass eye.

This was the end of Elizabeth's dream of becoming a surgeon. Surgeons had to have good eyesight. She no longer did. Yet Elizabeth did not give up. She knew she could still be a good doctor and help people in other ways.

In October 1850, Elizabeth moved from Paris to London. She began working at

St. Bartholomew's hospital. There, she met a young lady named Florence Nightingale. Elizabeth and Florence became friends at once. They had many things in common. Florence wanted to have a **career** (kuh-REER) in medicine, too, but her parents would not allow it. Elizabeth encouraged her friend to keep trying. Eventually, Florence's parents gave their permission. She became one of the best known nurses of all time. Elizabeth and Florence stayed friends throughout the rest of their lives.

Florence Nightingale is one of the most famous nurses of all time. This statue in London honors her work in the Crimean War.

FLORENCE NIGHTINGALE O M

FRANK LESLIE'S ILLUSTRATED NEWSPAPER

No. 759—Vol. XXX.]   NEW YORK, APRIL 16, 1870.   [Price, 10 Cents.

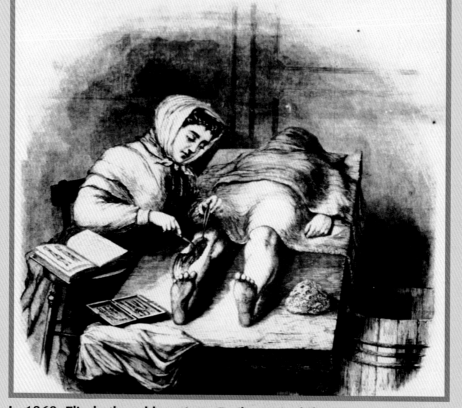

In 1868, Elizabeth and her sister Emily opened the Women's Medical College in New York. On April 16, 1870, they were featured in *Frank Leslie's Illustrated*, an important newspaper of this time period.

Helping Those In Need

In 1851, Elizabeth moved back to New York. She wanted to help **immigrants** (IH-mih-grunts) who were sick but could not pay for help. She started a free clinic on the Lower East Side of Manhattan. It was called the New York Infirmary (in-FIR-mer-ee) for **Indigent** (IN-dih-jent) Women and Children. All the doctors who worked there were women. The patients were all women and children, too.

Elizabeth believed that it was important to take care of the body. She knew that if people ate good food and stayed clean, they would not get sick as often. We know this is important today, but not many people in the 1800s knew about good **hygiene** (HY-jeen). Elizabeth tried to teach these things to people in her clinics.

Elizabeth had chosen a career over marriage. She was happy about her choice, yet sometimes she was lonely. She knew that many children were lonely too, so she decided to adopt a child. She found a little girl at an **orphanage** (OR-fuh-nidj) named Katharine "Kitty" Barry. Elizabeth raised Kitty as her own daughter.

Kitty always called Elizabeth "Doctor." One time, a doctor friend of Elizabeth's came to visit.

Elizabeth adopted Katharine "Kitty" Barry when Kitty was only seven years old. They had three pet dogs, Don, Burr, and Jack.

Kitty was very puzzled by this man. She asked Elizabeth, "Doctor, how very odd it is to hear a man called Doctor!" Elizabeth thought this was very funny. It also made her happy. Not many years before, it would have been odd to hear someone call a woman "Doctor." Now, because of what Elizabeth had achieved, children would grow up knowing that both men and women could have this job.

In 1861, the Civil War started in the United States. One reason for this war was slavery. The North thought that slavery should be ended. The South wanted to keep their slaves. Elizabeth wanted to help the North fight against slavery. The best way she could do that was by providing medical service.

Elizabeth helped train nurses and take care of wounded soldiers. She set up the United States Sanitary Commission. This improved the conditions at the military hospitals. The commission also helped the soldiers get better food and hygiene.

After the war, Elizabeth started a medical college for women. Her sister, Emily, had become a doctor too. They wanted to give other women the chance to learn about medicine. The Women's Medical College of the New York Infirmary opened in 1868. It trained many women to become doctors.

Because of her success in America, Elizabeth was asked to help women in England. Very few women there could get a medical education. They weren't allowed to attend the same schools as men.

Elizabeth chose to go to England. In 1875, she started teaching at the London School of Medicine for Women.

Elizabeth kept practicing medicine until she was seventy-three. She visited her family in the United States one last time when she was eighty-five years old.

In 1910, Kitty and Elizabeth took a vacation to Scotland. While there, Elizabeth fell down a staircase and was hurt. She never recovered. She died on May 31, 1910. Kitty was by her side. Elizabeth was buried in a small village in Scotland.

The final resting place of Elizabeth Blackwell is marked with a Celtic (KEL-tik) cross. She was buried at Saint Mun's Churchyard in Kilmun, Scotland.

Elizabeth Blackwell helped people everywhere. Because of her achievements, doors have been opened for women that were once closed. She showed that men and women can do anything they put their minds to. Her example has helped many people fulfill their dreams.

CHRONOLOGY

1821 Elizabeth Blackwell is born in Bristol, England, on February 3.

1832 Her family moves to America. They live in New York and New Jersey.

1838 The family moves to Cincinnati, Ohio. Samuel Blackwell dies.

1845 Elizabeth decides to become a doctor.

1847 She starts school at Geneva Medical College.

1849 She graduates head of her class. She moves to Paris to study surgery. After a serious eye infection, she loses one of her eyes.

1850 She becomes friends with Florence Nightingale.

1851 Elizabeth returns to New York.

1853 She opens a clinic in New York for poor women and children.

1854 She adopts Kitty Barry.

1861 Elizabeth trains nurses during the Civil War.

1868 She and her sister Emily open Women's Medical College of the New York Infirmary.

1869 Elizabeth returns to England to help women become doctors there.

1875 She starts teaching at the London School of Medicine for Women.

1894 She retires from medical practice.

1906 She makes her last trip to the United States to visit her family.

1910 Elizabeth dies on May 31.

TIMELINE IN HISTORY

1775 Revolutionary War begins; it will last until 1783.

1836 The Battle of the Alamo is fought in San Antonio, Texas.

1843 People start moving west on the Oregon Trail.

1848 Gold is discovered in California. Gold rush begins.

1860 Abraham Lincoln is elected president of the United States. The Civil War begins.

1863 Lincoln issues Emancipation Proclamation, which frees the slaves.

1865 Civil War ends. Thirteenth Amendment to the Constitution abolishes slavery. Louis Pasteur proposes that infection is caused by bacteria in open flesh. Joseph Lister uses carbolic acid to fight infection.

1868 Fourteenth Amendment gives U.S. citizenship to all African American men.

1870 African American men gain the right to vote.

1876 Alexander Graham Bell invents the telephone.

1878 Robert Koch uses steam to kill germs on medical instruments.

1893 The Johns Hopkins University Medical School (first modern American medical school) opens in Baltimore.

1914 World War I begins; it will last until 1918.

1916 Polio epidemics break out in New York and Boston; polio outbreaks will continue for decades to come.

1918 An influenza pandemic kills 15 million people worldwide, including 600,000 Americans.

1920 Women gain the right to vote.

1929 Stock market crashes. Great Depression begins.

1939 World War II begins; it will last until 1945.

1950 Korean War begins.

1959 Vietnam War begins; it will last until 1975.

1969 U.S. lands a man on the moon.

1997 Eighteen people in Hong Kong are infected with avian flu.

2001 Terrorists attack New York City and Washington, D.C.

2007 Sophie Currier, a Harvard medical student, wins a court case against the National Board of Medical Examiners after it refused to allow her to take extra break time during her exam in order to breast-feed her infant daughter.

FIND OUT MORE

Books

Binns, Tristan Boyer. *Elizabeth Blackwell: First Woman Physician.* New York: Franklin Watts, 2005.

Kishel, Ann-Marie. *Elizabeth Blackwell: A Life of Diligence.* Minneapolis, MN: Lerner Books, 2007.

LeClair, Mary K. "Tireless Healer." *Appleseeds.* March 2003, pp. 16–18.

Peck, Ira. *Elizabeth Blackwell: The First Woman Doctor.* Brookfield, Connecticut: Millbrook Press, 2000.

Works Consulted

Blackwell, Elizabeth. *Pioneer Work for Women.* New York: E.P. Dutton & Co., 1895.

"Daughters of Harvard." *Time.* October 9, 1944.
http://www.time.com/time/magazine/article/0,9171,803367,00.html

McFerran, Ann. *Elizabeth Blackwell, First Woman Doctor.* New York: Grosset & Dunlap, 1966.

National Library of Medicine: *Celebrating America's Women Physicians.* "Changing the Face of Medicine: Dr. Elizabeth Blackwell."
http://www.nlm.nih.gov/changingthefaceofmedicine/physicians/biography_35.html

Sahli, Nancy Ann. *Elizabeth Blackwell, M.D. (1821–1910): A Biography.* Philadelphia: University of Pennsylvania, 1974.

Stevenson, Keira. "Elizabeth Blackwell." Great Neck Publishing, 2005.

"Women Doctors." *Time Magazine*, April 24, 1933.
http://www.time.com/time/magazine/article/0,9171,769803,00.html

"Women Doctors." *Time Magazine*, January 13, 1941.
http://www.time.com/time/magazine article/0,9171,772566,00.html

On the Internet

Hobart and William Smith Colleges: Elizabeth Blackwell, MD
http://campus.hws.edu/his/blackwell/

National Library of Medicine: *History of Medicine*, "Elizabeth Blackwell, America's First Woman M.D"
http://www.nlm.nih.gov/hmd/blackwell/

Florence Nightingale
http://www.florence-nightingale.co.uk/flo2.htm

GLOSSARY

abolitionist (aa-buh-LIH-shuh-nist)—A person who believed slavery should be outlawed.

career (kuh-REER)—The type of job a person is trained to do and does for a long time.

clinic (KLIH-nik)—A place that gives medical treatment.

determined (dee-TER-mihnd)—Willing to work hard to reach a goal.

diploma (dih-PLOH-muh)—A certificate given to students who have completed all their classes in school.

graduation (grad-joo-WAY-shun)—A ceremony that honors students who have finished school. This is where they receive their diplomas.

hygiene (HY-jeen)—The practice of keeping clean to stay healthy.

immigrants (IH-mih-grunts)—People who move to a new country.

indigent (IN-dih-jent)—Poor.

medicine (MEH-dih-sin)—The science of identifying and treating diseases; also, the treatments for diseases.

opinions (oh-PIN-yuns)—What one thinks about something or somebody.

orphanage (OR-fuh-nidj)—A place where children live whose parents have died.

slavery (SLAY-vree)—The practice of owning people.

surgeon (SUR-jun)—A doctor who operates on sick or injured people to help them get better.

INDEX